Write It Right

Writing a Review

By Cecilia Minden and Kate Roth

Published in the United States of America by
Cherry Lake Press
Ann Arbor, Michigan, 2395 South Huron Parkway, Suite 200
www.cherrylakepublishing.com

Reading Adviser: Marla Conn, MS, Ed., Literacy specialist, Read-Ability, Inc.
Book Designer: Felicia Macheske
Character Illustrator: Carol Herring

Photo Credits: © risteski goce/Shutterstock.com, 7; © CGN089/Shutterstock.com, 11; © Brian A Smith/Shutterstock.com, 13; © ESB Professional/Shutterstock.com, 17; © Monkey Business Images/Shutterstock.com, 19; © Alena Ozerova/Shutterstock.com, 21

Graphics Throughout: © simple surface/Shutterstock.com; © Mix3r/Shutterstock.com; © Artefficient/Shutterstock.com; © lemony/Shutterstock.com; © Svetolk/Shutterstock.com; © EV-DA/Shutterstock.com; © briddy/Shutterstock.com; © IreneArt/Shutterstock.com

Library of Congress Cataloging-in-Publication Data

Names: Minden, Cecilia, author. | Roth, Kate, author. | Herring, Carol, illustrator.
Title: Writing a review / by Cecilia Minden and Kate Roth ; illustrated Carol Herring.
Description: Ann Arbor, Michigan : Cherry Lake Publishing, 2020. | Series: Write it right | Includes bibliographical references and index. | Audience: Grades 2-3
Identifiers: LCCN 2019033441 (print) | LCCN 2019033442 (ebook) | ISBN 9781534159068 (hardcover) | ISBN 9781534161368 (paperback) | ISBN 9781534160217 (pdf) | ISBN 9781534162518 (ebook)
Subjects: LCSH: Report writing–Juvenile literature.
Classification: LCC PE1478 .M56 2020 (print) | LCC PE1478 (ebook) | DDC 808.06–dc23
LC record available at https://lccn.loc.gov/2019033441
LC ebook record available at https://lccn.loc.gov/2019033442

Cherry Lake Publishing would like to acknowledge the work of the Partnership for 21st Century Learning, a Network of Battelle for Kids. Please visit *www.battelleforkids.org/networks/p21* for more information.

Printed in the United States of America
Corporate Graphics

Cherry Lake Press

Table of
CONTENTS

CHAPTER ONE

How Do You Decide?

Every day, you are bombarded with choices. On TV, on your smartphone, on your computer, and in every store window are ads encouraging you to spend your money. How do you make the best choice?

Consumers buy **products**. **Reviews** are written by people who have tried out the product. Music, movies, books, and food are a few of the things people review. Reviews give consumers the information they need to decide which products to buy.

Your **opinion** counts! You can help others by learning to write a good review.

Here's what you'll need to complete the activities in this book:

- Pencil
- Paper

ACTIVITY

Choose the Product

In this activity, you will make a list of things you could review.

INSTRUCTIONS:

1. Make a list of products you use that you could review.
2. Include products you use often and really like or dislike.
3. Choose one to review.

Sample Activity

- Luigi's cheeseburger pizza
- Sully's Organic Dog Treats
- Timorama tube socks ✓
- *The Case of the Lost Dinosaur*, a mystery book

A good review encourages others to buy a product.

CHAPTER TWO

What Does It Do?

When you review a product, you need to tell readers all about it. First, you need to give a **description** of the product. What is its purpose? What does the product look like? What is the size and color? What is its shape? How does it look and feel? What else do you think a person reading your review might want to know?

ACTIVITY

Describe the Product

In this activity, you will practice describing a product.

INSTRUCTIONS:

1. Describe the purpose of the product. Why did you buy it? What will you use it for?
2. Describe what the product looks like.

Sample Product Description

I love wearing socks with cool designs on them. They help show my personality. But I noticed my usual socks get duller with each wash. Sometimes they even get holes in them—or worse, they shrink! Last week, I bought a pair of Timorama tube socks. They have dinosaurs on them! They have other cool designs too. They are made in the USA. A pair costs $5.99.

CHAPTER THREE

Will This Work?

Take time to **evaluate** the product you are reviewing. Try out all of the **features**. For example, if you are reviewing dog treats, give one to your dog to see if he likes it. You may want to ask your vet if the treat is good for your dog.

Once you've tried out the product, decide if it works the way you think it should. Is there something about the product that doesn't work correctly? What would you change about the product? In your opinion, what is great about the product? Is it something you will keep using? Is the product worth the price you paid for it?

Make sure the product meets all your needs.

ACTIVITY

Evaluate the Product

In this activity, you will add a paragraph to your review. It will explain your evaluation of the product.

INSTRUCTIONS:

1. Write a paragraph to share your evaluation of the product.
2. Answer these questions:
   a. What are the best and worst features of the product?
   b. Does the product work the way you think it should?
   c. Is there anything about the product you would change?
   d. Is the price of the product fair?
3. Use details to support your ideas.

Sample Product Evaluation

Timorama tube socks are made in the USA. They have fun designs like aliens and pizza slices. They come in all kinds of colors and patterns. They are perfect for someone like me, but they may not be for someone who doesn't like wearing colorful socks. They stay bright and colorful after each wash, and they never shrink! The price is a little high at $5.99 a pair. I wish they offered bundled packs of four or six pairs at a discounted rate. That way, I could collect more cool designs.

Keep a running list of your reactions as you review the product.

CHAPTER FOUR

Which One Do I Choose?

We can compare things we like to **similar** products. That way, we can decide which one we like best. For example, you may like one brand of frozen pizza more than another. Reviews compare products that are similar. They explain how one product is better or worse than another and why. This can help give consumers a good understanding of the products. They can pick the one that has the features they like best.

Compare your product to another product to give your readers a clearer picture.

ACTIVITY

Compare the Product

In this activity, you will add a paragraph to compare the product to others that are similar.

INSTRUCTIONS:

1. Write a paragraph to compare the product to other products.
2. Answer these questions:
    a. Have you used a product that is similar?
    b. How is the product you are reviewing better or worse than others you have used?
3. Use details to support your ideas.

Sample Product Comparison

I used to buy regular tube socks, but they didn't last well after a wash. They usually lost their color after a couple of weeks. Sometimes they would shrink or get holes in them. I even tried waiting until the last moment to wash them. But my mom didn't like that. She said they stank. Timorama tube stocks stay bright and colorful!

CHAPTER FIVE

Your Final Choice

End your review with your **recommendations**. This means you tell others whether or not they should buy the product. Try to be fair. Consider the good and bad points you discovered. If you didn't like the product, explain why you did not like it. If you liked the product, point out what makes it special.

A person reading your review might make a decision based on what you say. Ask yourself if you could make a decision based on your review.

Be sure to write an honest review.
Others are depending on your observations.

ACTIVITY

Recommendations

In this activity, you will write the last paragraph of your review. This is where you will make your recommendations.

INSTRUCTIONS:

1. Write a paragraph to tell others whether they should buy this product or not. Answer these questions:
   a. Should someone buy this product? Why or why not?
   b. What is the product good for?
   c. Who will like the product?
2. Use details to support your ideas.

Sample Review

I would recommend Timorama tube socks to anyone who likes fun designs. The price is a little high, but the quality of the socks is so much better than other products. They don't shrink or lose their bright colors in the wash. I'm really excited to buy my next pair. I think I'll get the robot ones next!

Make sure to check with an adult before posting your review online.

CHAPTER SIX

Tell Others All About It

Now you can share your review with others. Maybe they will buy a product based on your review. What would you like to review next?

Get others to write reviews and trade ideas about products.

ACTIVITY

Take a Final Look!

Ask yourself these questions as you reread your review:

- Did I choose a product that I know a lot about?
- Did I describe it with a lot of details?
- Did I evaluate the product fairly?
- Did I compare it to other products that do similar things?
- Did I make a final recommendation of whether someone should buy it or not?
- Did I use correct grammar and spelling?

GLOSSARY

consumers (kuhn-SOO-murz) people who buy and use products

description (dih-SKRIP-shuhn) words that create a picture of something in the mind of a person who reads or hears them

evaluate (ih-VAL-yoo-ate) to decide the value of something

features (FEE-churz) particular parts or qualities of a person, place, or thing

opinion (uh-PIN-yuhn) a personal feeling or belief about someone or something

products (PRAH-duhkts) things that are made and sold

recommendations (rek-uh-men-DAY-shuhnz) suggestions that are good or worthwhile about a product

reviews (rih-VYOOZ) pieces of writing that give opinions about books, movies, or products

similar (SIM-uh-lur) having many features in common

For More

INFORMATION

BOOKS

Kamberg, *Mary-Lane.* The I Love to Write Book: Ideas & Tips for Young Writers. Milwaukee, WI: Crickhollow Books, 2008.

Olien, Rebecca. *Kids Write! Fantasy & Sci Fi, Mystery, Autobiography, Adventure, and More!* Nashville, TN: Williamson Books, 2005.

WEBSITES

Scholastic–Share What You're Reading!
http://teacher.scholastic.com/activities/swyar/browse.asp
See what kids your age are reading and check out their reviews.
You can even add your own review!

Spaghetti Book Club–Book Reviews by Kids for Kids
www.spaghettibookclub.org
Check out this site to read book reviews and submit your own reviews.

INDEX

About the AUTHORS

Cecilia Minden is the former director of the Language and Literacy Program at Harvard Graduate School of Education. She earned her doctorate from the University of Virginia. While at Harvard, Dr. Minden also taught several writing courses. Her research focused on early literacy skills and developing phonics curriculums. She is now a literacy consultant and the author of over 200 books for children. Dr. Minden lives with her family in McKinney, Texas. She enjoys helping students become interested in reading and writing.

Kate Roth has a doctorate from Harvard University in language and literacy and a master's degree from Columbia University Teachers College in curriculum and teaching. Her work focuses on writing instruction in the primary grades. She has taught kindergarten, first grade, and Reading Recovery. She has also instructed hundreds of teachers from around the world in early literacy practices. She lived with her husband and three children in China for many years, and now they live in Connecticut.